Stygian

Alexandra Requena

BookLeaf Publishing

India | USA | UK

Presentation by *BookLeaf Publishing*

Web: www.bookleafpub.com

E-mail: info@bookleafpub.com

ISBN: 9789357215008

First edition 2022

I want to dedicate this book to my mom, she has always been my number one supporter and without her I wouldn't have come as far as I did. Thank you.

Stained Winter Wonderland

The cool crisp winter air, beats me like a drum.
My coat is open, as I cry.
Scarves and gloves are long forgotten, as well as
my memories.
Why am I here? How did I get here?
Please, leave me alone-

let me run away.

Running through a crowd, I feel small
snowflakes hit my face.
I have no idea where I am, or why I am here-
yet I know I need to escape.
A voice calls for me in the distance, trying,
attempting to get me to follow, but-

I just run. Run far away.

Just let me go home.

Desperation and desolation are my only
companions
as I fight for what once was mine.
I have lost all control of my thoughts,
I feel little and damaged.

                              "Mind,
please come back!

Help me get home!"

My pleads drowned by the howling wind,
as the cold takes one more victim.

Wonderful Creatures

The flutter of these black wings that cover your
eyes won't seem to stop.
How do I wish to grasp the attention of these
wonderful creatures.

My life is just a pure mirage in everyone's eyes.
Aren't the pretty delusions of human beings
such wonderful creatures?

Back and forth like the tides on the beach from
my childhood town, memories come and go.
Oh don't I wish I could go back to when we
were such wonderful creatures.

Everything in life seems like a distant voice,
such a blur,
How can I expect happiness if I haven't
immersed myself with these wonderful
creatures?

Memories are just made of dust and weakness,
Yet again these are what makes us wonderful
creatures

One can only see as much as you allow them of
your soul,
Here we lie again, two wonderful creatures.

I wonder what our hearts mumble to each other,
lying so close.
What would they have to say about these
wonderful creatures?

In the privacy of my mind, I stare into your soul.
I have been trapped by the gaze of those
wonderful creatures.

Yet again I have to let go and leave.
My heart aching and longing for my wonderful
creatures.

Loneliness seems to overcome my once sane
mind.
Oh how I think of your eyes, being wild but
wonderful creatures.

The flutter of these black wings that cover your
eyes won't seem to stop.
How do I wish to grasp the attention of these
wonderful creatures.

Fear

Wind Gushes
Heart Beats
Tears Fall
You and I
We pray

Postal Return

Seasons come and go,
I sit by my window,
watching.
One thing never changes,
the letter that sits on my table
RETURN TO SENDER.
But you are gone,
and I cannot thrive
in a world where your laughter isn't present
you wine isn't consumed
and your walks aren't accompanied.
I wear red,
daily,
To remind myself of you.

Frustration

Bang
Crash
Thud
Toss
Get rid of it all
Emotions rush
Your face flushes red
Scream
Cry
Whine
Pout
Stomp
Head spinning
Heart beating
Finally, free.

Dream

Succumb to slumber
Let it go.
Isn't it interesting,
how humans memorize things?
We lock in chamber,
doze off the day,
Memories solidify
subconscious mind.

Human Expectations

I expect the moon in the sky,
but how dare I be an empath?
I expect love, kindness,
but how dare I love myself?
The tree is expected to grow,
The weather to change,
But how dare I do the same?
Yet, when it comes to human relations,
I am taught to have no expectations,
accept whoever comes,
care for the fallen.
But who cares for me?

New Risings

She raised her hands to the sun
wax melting
then sat there
eyes filled with tears
wondering
why she had never learnt
to fly.

Home

Trees grow
Leaves fall
Roots dig deep into the soil.
It's permanent,
Reminiscent of the past.
You look at the big blue house,
In hopes of getting a glimpse of who you once
were.
But home has changed,
And so have you.

Distorted View

I snack
I stare
Wishing to cut with scissors
What doesn't belong.
My extremities are too long
My head too big
My stomach sticks out.
I sigh
And the cycle repeats.

Future

In this world
there are people who reach their palms
to the sky
reach high and dream big.
Look at the sky,
you can't expect to be any more
than a spec in the universe.

Love

I am a bird,
seeking for a nest,
being embraced
in the arms of the wind.

Childhood

If fairy tales are real
If fairy tales teach
We must learn that we
Fall in love with
Short stories
Dynamic progress
And
dreams.

Secret

Hush little baby,
don't say a word
screaming matches are all heard.
And if that mockingbird don't sing
daddy's gonna make sure that his words sting.
And if that diamond ring is glass,
you find your only self-worth in class.
And if that looking glass gets broke,
bullies are going to tear and poke.
Hush little baby,
don't say a word
someday you'll rule the world.

Elements

I am fire,

bold enough
to fight life
soft enough
to light the way.

Strength

18

I have a shell,
only the faintest can break it.

I am Woman

I AM WOMAN
Woman with words,
a book
and pen
can move the world.

Woman with strength
mind
and will
can do anything.

Wonder

Waves kiss the shore,
trees reach for the sky,
seasons change,
people will come and go.
Nothing remains the same,
in a time that changes by the second.
So when life tells you,
"Let go and be free"
you must have the courage to do so.

No Man's Return

A place no one knows
where life doesn't move the same,
time stops
and wings grow.
A place that is peaceful,
where bad luck has no chance.
Sights to be seen,
love to be felt.
Voids filled.
A place not worth leaving.
At the end of the line,
we reach bliss,
and visit
No Man's Return.

Human Emotion

We are all so different
but we live many of the same life experiences.
One way or another,
we all experience pain.
No one,
nothing matters,
only the person,
in front,
with gloomy eyes,
such as your own.

Culmination

In life
        all the experiences
                form who you are
                        regardless of good or
bad.
Does it really matter
        the effort you've put in
                to be different?
We're all just the same,
        following the path of life
                searching and yearning
                        for what will bring us
peace.